Stock Market

A N D

Foreign Exchange Market

An Empirical Guidance

IAN CHARLES ROBERT GRACIAS

ISBN: 978-1-4834-7072-6 (sc)
ISBN: 978-1-4834-7071-9 (e)

Library of Congress Control Number: 2017908442

Lulu Publishing Services rev. date: 12/5/2017

Dedication for this book.

I dedicate this book to my mother Marina Eugenia Nita Gracias, and late father Maurice Joseph Manoel Gracias who both encouraged me to keep studying at any age and follow my dream, I would not be the person i am today if it were not for their support and encouragement. They often reminded me that dreams can turn to reality, so make it happen.

Acknowledgements

I would like to thanks the following people :

The Daily FX educational department – Jeremy Wagner ,Richard Krivo, James Stanley, and Tom Long, I had initially learnt about trading the Forex markets, which gave the initial interest in Finance.

FX Trader's EDGE – Jody Samuels - I took the flagship Elliott Wave Ultimate Course.

While doing the course, it gave me the confidence and motivation to trade the Forex markets, and to study for a Masters Degree in Finance, which finally resulted in this book.

Mrs Pooja Jai Anam – CFA Institute India

DR . Jaspreet Kaur
Asst Professor,
Dayalbagh Educational Institute,
Agra
India

Both had helped me in the journey of subject Finance.

Mohamed Hoque my first Finance tutor who supported me in my understanding of all subjects of Finance.

Contents

Abstract

This book evaluates the relationship between the stock markets and exchange rate markets in the United Kingdom and in the United States of America. In order to determine the relationship between the FTSE 100 index and the NASDAQ 100 index, the regression between the independent and dependent variables has been used. The results revealed that the relationship of FTSE returns was seen with all the exchange rates against GBP, but the extent of relationship was strong only in three currencies: GBP/AUD, GBP/YEN, and GBP/CAD. Similarly, the relationship of NASDAQ 100 returns with those of currencies against GBP was found to be strong in three currencies and weak with other three currencies. It was seen that an asset market approach was found to be relevant in the models where a strong exchange rate relationship with stock returns was seen.

Introduction

Different studies show a variety of relationships between stock markets and foreign exchange markets. Foreign exchange markets and stock markets are two different aspects and factors that are controlled not by a single factor but by various direct and indirect factors. These two are found to play a significant role, both toward the investors and building the economy strong.

The investors in the stock market trade in different securities, where the investments are derived from various other factors, influencing the stock prices. The exchange rate market is a currency mechanism, whereas the stock market is a place but need not be a physical place where shares are bought and sold. The stock markets are highly regulated by the regulators, whereas the exchange rates do not experience the similar regulatory mechanism. Additionally, the stock markets are mainly affected by the market factors, firm factors, and other regulatory factors. On the contrary, the exchange rates are mainly influenced by the economic indicators that directly or indirectly affect the performance and operation of exchange rates. In other words, there is no strong and stable mechanism that has a control monopoly over the movement of exchange rates. Because the economy comprises two basic indicators (namely, exchange rate and stock markets) that directly or indirectly enhance the economic growth of the country, the in-depth relationship can be understood by examining the functioning of these two factors and their relationship. Hence it becomes important to examine the understanding of this relationship, which can enhance the returns to both the investors and the economy.

Stock Market

The stock market is a medium where buying and selling of shares or stocks are carried out (Buehler and Kohut 2006). These can be divided into components—namely, primary market and secondary market. In the primary market, new securities are issued by the company through IPO, private placement, in order to obtain funds from the public. Specifically, institutional investors are major players in this market. When shares are traded multiple times, those are said to be in the secondary market. In this, both institutional investors and individuals are major players. The two largest stock markets are the New York Stock Exchange and the NASDAQ. As trade has developed technologically, shares are traded in the electronic form in these markets, especially in the NASDAQ.

From a firm's perspective, the stock market is a source of generating funds for the firm. For example, if the firm wants to implement its strategic planning for the coming three years and is in immediate need of funds to execute this strategy, then for this purpose, the firm has different options to collect the funds. The financial institutions offer and provide different types of loans and financial incentives, the venture capitalists may be reached for obtaining loan facility, and the firm can also access stock markets for generating funds for the new project. These stock markets help in getting funds from diverse investors, who can be existing shareholders or the new ones. For this process, a firm should be registered in the stock exchange.

The shares are traded on the exchanges where they are listed. This trade includes the buying and selling by varied customers, who customize their needs for investment. The trading of the shares is done depending on the needs of investors. The point on which to focus is the determination of the prices of the stocks, which is further determined by many factors, primarily demand and supply. This demand and supply is seen as orders that flow in the stock market, where bid and ask prices are executed. The consideration is of what factors affect this order flow (i.e., the demand and supply).

Also, in order to trade in the international markets, the firm has to have ADRs and GDRs, where its share becomes available to global customers. This enables the firms to obtain capital from global markets.

The stock market is assumed to be efficient, where the information can be seen from the behavior of the investors. Taking this in technical terms, the efficient market hypothesis explains that the prices are affected by the information available in the market. This information is seen in different aspects, which can be related to gross domestic product, trade balance of the country, inflation rates, interest rates, price level, and money supply in the economy. This information affects the sentiments of the investors, trading in domestic as well as international markets. The transactions done according to these sentiments somewhere affect the exchange rate markets, where it is seen to include both direct trade in the currency market and the reserves of the central bank of the country.

In the macro view, during the recent crises of 2007–2008, it was seen that stock markets plummeted to an all-time low, causing investors to fear losing their money. This caused the withdrawals from the markets, resulting in capital outflow. The impact was seen on other factors that operate in the economy, like foreign reserves depletion and an increase in deficit in current account (CAD) of the country, trapping the economy in the vicious circle.

The central banks of developed economies do play a role in determining the stock market changes. The stock market is all about the sentiments of the investors, and whenever there are changes in any factor, its effect could easily be seen in the order flows in stock market. This proves the existence of the efficient market hypothesis (EMH). A recent case of the relationship between the foreign exchange rate and stock market was seen. The GBP began to improve because of the housing market in the UK. The mortgage approval increased, which caused the government to increase the lending rate; this led to an increase in the investments in GBP and hence in the LSE, where stock markets started to improve.

It has also been seen that stock market is a function of various macro- and microeconomic factors. If the stock market plummets, investors would move to minimize opportunity cost, resulting in fall in demand for money—hence low interest rates in the economy—further resulting in outflow of capital. Therefore, there would be a fall in the value of the currency (Aggarwal 1981).

Foreign Exchange Market

Trading foreign currencies represents the foreign exchange market. Globally, every country has its own currency, which is used as a medium for buying and selling goods and services in the country. By using the medium of currency, exchange of value is carried out, which is inbuilt to currency and goods, which is exchanged for the value of money. Because the currency has its value and is tradable as well, this has enabled buyers and sellers to develop and establish a market for carrying out the sale and purchase of currencies. Moreover, it is relevant to highlight that currency applicable to one country cannot be used as a medium of exchange in another country. For example, the US dollar cannot be freely used as a medium of exchange in the United Kingdom, but the value of trade with regard to sterling can be used for the purpose of buying and selling.

Based on this premise, the foreign exchange market facilitates different types of trading activities: spot rate, swap, forward rate, future, and option (Glantz and Kissell 2014). Spot rate, which is also known as the current exchange rate, mainly takes place in the form of cash transaction, necessitating exchange of value through buying and selling of currency. Swap is an agreement for exchanging currencies for the predetermined amount of time and subsequently reversing the deal at the end of mentioned time period; it is mostly carried out over the counter: Forward rate reflects an agreement between contracting parties for entering into a contractual relationship through making a transaction for a predetermined foreign exchange rate at a particular time in future. Future is also similar to the forward contract, but it mostly uses a three-month time frame for execution of agreement. An option contract gives an opportunity to investors to buy the right to exchange one type of currency with another type of currency at a predetermined time and predetermined foreign exchange value (Glantaz and Kissell 2014).

Based on the these descriptions, it is worth mentioning that time and exchange rate value are two important components in the foreign exchange market. Subsequently, it is at the will and wish of negotiating parties to determine value and exchange rate value for carrying out their agreement conditions.

Extending further, the determination of exchange rate also contributes to the understanding of this kind of relationship. Different approaches of determination of equilibrium exchange rate explain the different relationships between stock prices and exchange rates. The portfolio balance model demonstrates the equilibrium rate through the interaction between demand and supply of assets, which can include currencies portfolios. An increase in the price of any asset (say, stock prices) would affect the wealth of an individual, causing the demand of that asset being higher and hence lowering the price of other asset. This can be seen in world portfolio investment, where change in stock prices would impact the demand and supply and hence the exchange rate. Further, the asset market approach (Branson 1983) explains the equilibrium exchange rate is determined by demand and supply of stocks and bonds. It explains that because of change in exchange rate, the asset prices change, and hence the stock prices change. If the value of that currency changes, then the value of that asset also changes, exposing the individual to exchange rate risk. Furthermore, the CAPM of exchange rate risk to a firm, when studied in context of cross-borders, can contribute in understanding the exchange rate risk and comovement with global market portfolio. In simpler terms, the theory explains that firms consider investing in foreign currencies so that higher returns can be obtained and risks can be minimized. In order to create a risk-free and more profitable capital structure, firms are seen to continuously diversify their portfolios. They invest in different profitable forms of security and enhance their capital asset values. As the capital assets values of firms enhance, the entire economy of a nation experiences growth and development. Interest rates surge, and the appreciation of currency values is affected (Dornbusch 1976).

It has been seen that currency market is influenced by equity market in many cases. Suppose the indices at the London Stock Exchanges show excellent gains. The foreign investors would plunge their money in GDRs in LSE, or directly. This would give strength to sterling, improving the economic status of the country, with increases foreign reserves. On the other hand, the converse will happen if the equity market falls.

Therefore, there is no particular consensus on the relationship between the two variables. The study aims to develop strong evidence, where modeling of such a relationship explains the investing decisions of firms and hence adds value to the wealth of the shareholder.

Literature Review

Effects of Operations of Stock Market on the Operations of Foreign Exchange Market, and Vice Versa

Various theories have provided their perspectives on the relationship between stock market indices and exchange rate markets. The relationship between stock market and exchange market has been largely mixed. Franck and Young (1972) contended that there exists no substantial relationship between stock market and exchange rate dynamics. Based on this perspective, it can be deduced that the findings of Franck and Young did not provide ample and strong evidence reflecting any substantial relationship between the variables operational in both markets. In this regard, it is important to mention that they have mentioned the word *substantial* for determining the strength of the relationship. In other words, their perspective reflects that the strength of the relationship between stock market and exchange market has been weak; this can be a reasonable deduction from Franck and Young's findings. As a result, it is difficult to fully agree with this position and perspective.

The study of Dornbusch and Fisher (1980) highlighted that the changes in the currency movements directly affect the real output of the country, which subsequently put its influence on the future cash flows and on the performance of stock prices. However, this perspective looks a macro view of the relationship by highlighting the transmission effect, starting from the place of currency changes and their ultimate effect on the future cash flows and stock prices. In this regard, it is pertinent to highlight that the exchange rate market has no direct relationship with the performance of stock market indices.

Subsequently, Aggarwal (1981) carried out a detailed study for ascertaining the relationship between the operational indices in the United States with the exchange rate of dollar. The findings revealed the existence of positive correlation between the exchange rate and indices; more specifically, he highlighted that the revaluation of the US dollar is directly attached to the returns of stock markets. In other words, this finding reveals the effects of the US dollar through foreign exchange markets have put their influence on the returns generated by the stock markets. In this regard, it is important to mention that the effect starts from the foreign exchange market and subsequently impacts the stock market. However, this perspective is only restricted to prove the relationship from the perspective of exchange markets to capital markets; it does not highlight the relationship from the stock market to exchange markets. The findings of both Franck and Young (1972) and Aggarwal (1981) represent two different perspectives on the topic. The former are fully convinced that there exists no relationship between them, whereas the latter was able to find a relationship between the two. This proves that the work of Franck and Young (1972) was insufficient to prove any relationship between these two indices. Additionally, during the time of Franck and Young, stock exchanges and foreign exchange markets were in their primitive phase; many fundamental variables in both markets were undergoing the process of evolution and development. More important, global oil crises also largely influenced the internal market sentiments of shareholders and traders working in these markets. For example, the 1970s experienced substantial political, economic, and financial instability due to the cold war between the United States and Russia, the Middle East oil crises, and the crash of the US stock market in 1972 and 1973. Those prime factors did not allow for smooth functioning of these markets during that period of time.

The impact of the stock (business sector) cost on exchange rate can be considered through incorporating exchanges in stocks in the money demand function. Alluding to the 1920s onset of the Great Depression in the United States, Field (1984) accentuates the significance of considering the huge effect of the worth of stock exchanging on the interest to hold money parities. He states that the truth of having not perceived stock exchanging as an applicable contention in the demand for money (a development of the cash supply could be misinterpreted as expansionary, whereas it may be nonpartisan, or even prohibitive, to be specific if rising turnover figures in resource advertises completely retain the extra liquidity) drove it by implication to the Great Depression. The way of fiscal approach was misconstrued and was less costly than the FED suspected. Thus, he joins money markets in his enlarged cash interest capacity—in particular, the exchange volume of stock exchanges reproduced by the stock cost.

In a cutting-edge rendition of the Field contention, one may contend for FDI that the interest for household cash increments if remote financial specialists put resources into residential ventures and raise the ostensible measure of securities exchange exchanges. From one viewpoint (stock cost increments), again the interest rate goes up in increments as a result of the expanded demand for money. Accordingly, capital inflows are supported, and household money will acknowledge under adaptable conversion standard. In the event of an altered conversion standard, stock exchange costs ought to subsequently have no impact on trade rates, however they may have an effect on remote trade stores of the national bank, which is focused on safeguarding the present estimation of the swapping scale. On the off chance that local cash admires, the national bank is obliged to perform remote trade intercessions. Clearly the swapping scale can have an effect on the stock cost at a smaller scale. Nonetheless, at the full-scale level, the effect could be weaker or even nonexistent, because a stock exchange list really measures the execution of a broadened portfolio. As it were, ventures (weighted by their capital stock) of a few commercial enterprises are fused in a securities exchange file. The conversion scale ought to have a more prominent effect on a securities exchange file when more fair arranged ventures are spoken to in a stocks list. Subsequently, the creation of a stock exchange record is an urgent insight concerning the inquiry regarding whether the swapping scale does in fact have a noteworthy effect on a money markets list.

At the full-scale level, capital inflows (e.g., because of interests in securities) can have an effect on the exchange rate. Interests in securities can be made either in bonds or in shares. Thus, exchange rates are not influenced only through foreign speculations on domestic securities, but also through remote ventures on recorded residential endeavors. As per the Capital Asset Pricing Model (CAPM), the speculator is willing to tolerate a higher danger on the off chance that he or she expects an undertaking return, which is at any rate as high as its relating beta (Sharpe et al. 1995). Subsequently, the security market line (SML) can be utilized to evaluate shares, and along these lines it is very much a helpful instrument in settling on choices for speculators.

Concerning the effects of the stock market on the foreign exchange market and vice versa, the historical findings of various researchers are worth critically examining. The stock prices are not significantly affected by the changes in the exchange rates (Solnik 1987). On the other hand, Soenen and Hennigan (1988) revealed negative relationship between the variables of the US dollar and stock prices registered in the stock markets of the United States; the study period was 1980–1986. Subsequently, a moderate relationship was found between US stock prices and the US dollar exchange rate from the period of 1971–1987 (Jorion 1990).

In this regard, it is important to mention that till that time, the researchers had only provided the relationship between the main variables (i.e., stock exchange and exchange rate) and had restricted their findings to the extent of the relationship between these two factors. However, these authors have failed to highlight and provide the effects of stock exchange on the exchange market, and vice versa. Under this situation, it would be highly difficult to rely on the findings provided by them because they have not provided results by highlighting the independent variable and dependent variable, which is a central theme for assessing a level of relationship.

Keeping this view in mind, the researcher will try to address this gap by determining and assigning independent and dependent variable status to variables in order to ascertain the effects of one variable on the other.

The application of classical economic theory provides a separate perspective on the relationship between stock prices and exchange rates. According to the classical economic theory, there exists a relationship between stock prices and exchanges within an economy. The flow-oriented model elucidates that movements of currency impacts the international competitiveness, trade balance, and real output of an economy, which in turn influence expected and future cash flows of firms and their share prices (Phylaktis and Ravazzolo 2005).

Based on this theory, it can be deduced that the stock prices are not directly affected by the changes in the exchange rates, but they are influenced by the economic activities taking place in the economy in which the firms produce goods and services, pay taxes, hire employees, design and develop new business strategies, and compete in the industry and the economy. Subsequently, when the actual or physical output is generated within the economy, which reflects the actual financial and operational performance of the economy and firms operating within the boundary of that economy, the net performance is depicted through revenue, gross profit, operating profit and net present value, price earnings ratio, dividend payout ratio, and other indicators reflecting the overall financial and business performance of the economy and the firms. At the same time, it is vital to highlight that both stock prices and exchange rates are forecasted and expected values commonly reflected through indices. More specifically, stock prices have been identified as sentiments of investors and shareholders buying and selling shares in the stock market. Overall, the equity market reflects the aggregate behavior of the market in which, if the equity marketing touches new psychological level by recording more points in the index, it would reflect that the majority of the market participants have developed positive and constructive sentiment relating to their investment in different stocks. In contrast, if the equity markets touch the lower lock position, this would indicate the majority shareholders and investors show less optimism about their investment, firm performance, and overall prospects. The same perspective is also relevant and applicable to exchange market, where buyers and sellers of currencies share their expectations, and the exchange market represents their perspective.

In addition, it has been argued that only in fully integrated financial markets is volatility of exchange rate associated with the stock price volatility (Zapatero 1995). In other words, the researcher has hinted that integration of full markets is a prerequisite for association between stock markets and exchange market. Within this context, because of faster deregulation and integration of the international financial markets, foreign exchange rates have also increased their sensitivity with regard to the stock market innovations (Yang and Doong 2004).

This point warrants further elaboration. First, integration has not been clearly elucidated by the research provided by Zapatero, making it hard for defining and determining the extent of functional relationship between capital markets and foreign exchange markets. However, the work of Yang and Doong has appropriately elaborated on the type of change that facilitates interaction between the capital markets and the foreign exchange markets. For example, they have mentioned that the deregulation of capital markets have played the role for mending and retaining the relationship between the two markets. More clearly, it can be deduced that the role of regulator, such as the London Stock Exchange (LSE), regulates the conduct of stock exchange through different regulatory measures. For example, the LSE provides different requirements and conditions that are necessary to be satisfied and fully submitted by any firm intending to register at the LSE. Additionally, if the LSE relaxes some of the rules for company registration, this action reflects that the LSE is deregulating, empowering, and encouraging the new and unregistered firms to avail this opportunity and participate in the stock market operations. In other words, when the application of deregulation is analyzed, it can be easily deduced that such leeway is similar to the one adopted in the exchange markets, where mostly contracts are carried out between buyers and sellers in which participants are given more rights and authorities to carry out their agreements.

The monetarist model of exchange rate determination also signifies correlation between stock markets and exchange markets. This model reflects that the equities are a part of wealth and affect the tendency of foreign exchange rates through raising demand for money (Gavin 1989). In other words, this model exhibits that the effects of stock markets will subsequently put influence on the foreign exchange markets, which will show their behavior according to the effects of the stock markets. In this regard, it is important to point out that in terms of capitalization, stock markets are higher than the capitalization in foreign exchange markets. This fact is mainly caused by the fact that various local and international firms are registered and operational in the stock markets, whereas only foreign currencies are traded in the foreign exchange markets.

The asset market approach has different perspective on this issue. Frankel (1983) contends the asset market approach highlights that changes in stock prices directly affect exchange rates because it is expected the financial asset price changes impact the exchange rate dynamism. In other words, it can be extracted that the asset market model is not indicating that causality effect starts from exchange rate to the stock market, but vice versa. On the other hand, some authors have found the relationship between exchange rate and stock price, in which effect starts from the exchange rate to the stock market. Dornbusch and Fisher (1980) reflect that the goods market approach posits that the causality effect first takes place in the exchange rate and then moves to stock prices.

The Difference between the Stock Market and the Foreign Exchange Market

Stock markets and exchange markets do not receive simultaneous influence from other variables. Simultaneous influence refers to experience of the same type and level of influence from the variables directly or indirectly associated with the stock markets and exchange markets. For example, the stock market is mainly influenced by the understanding of shareholders, investors, brokers, and stock market regulators, because they are ones who are directly involved in the sale and purchase of stocks in the market. At the same time, a firm's individual financial and operational performance, current and future strategic policies, and expectations of shareholders and investors are factors that are directly attached with the performance of stock markets.

On the other hand, buyers and sellers of currencies are not required to see the financial and business performance of companies, but they are more interested in observing and taking into account the economic performance and political factors of the related currencies. For example, unemployment rate and its effects on the US dollar are closely monitored by the various operators trading the US dollar, because the unemployment rate is generally considered the most effective economic indicator of the economic policies of the US government and the Federal Reserve. Based on this situation, it can be easily deduced that both stock markets and exchange rate markets have different variables that affect them and influence them separately.

More simply, in the stock markets, thousands of firms are registered in contrast to the foreign exchange markets, where a few hundred firms or individuals trade in the foreign currencies. Similarly, in the foreign exchange markets, only currencies and foreign exchange–related contracts, such as options, futures, and forward contracts are carried out. On the other hand, the stock markets facilitate the operation and trade of preference shares and ordinary shares of the firms. Additionally, the firms issue millions of shares, which are traded in the stock markets, whereas currencies are not issued by the firms but the government regulators, such as the Bank of England, and the currencies can only be used a commodity for buying and selling.

Within this context, it is important to highlight that the ownership of currencies does not change, but only control is given to the traders. For example, if a person sells five pounds and receives the value of five pounds, the seller has not sold the ownership of the currency but only value to the buyer. The same is also applicable to the buyer because he cannot claim ownership of the purchased currency. This is mainly caused by the fact that the ownership of currency is retained by the regulator, such as Bank of England or the government of United Kingdom.

In addition, frequency of transactions between stock markets and foreign exchange markets is considerably different. For example, stock markets have higher frequency than the foreign exchange markets because firms issue millions of shares, and the shareholders and investors regularly trade them. As shareholders and investors receive information from different sources and understand them in their own way, this enables them to adjust their positions by increasing their return or decreasing their loss, and by avoiding the risk of loss as well. In contrast, the frequency of foreign currencies is largely limited, and that is mainly caused by the comparatively limited number of traders and the tendency of foreign currency values.

For example, one of the important and main reasons behind less volatility in the foreign exchange market is the number of variables that directly influence the daily movement. More clearly, apart from the market sentiment and market information about the particular currency, the role of economic information puts substantial effect on the current and future trend of the foreign exchange markets. Since the currency-related variables are highly associated with the regulatory mechanism, it is plausible to expect lesser frequency in the values of foreign currency values. More significantly, in foreign exchange markets, one type of currency is given to buy another type of currency. For example, if one wants to buy the US dollar, he is required to pay pounds of equivalent value for buying the US dollar. In other words, it can be deduced that in the foreign exchange market, only currency values are traded and exchanged, whereas shares are bought in return of currency payment. This is the fundamental difference between activities taking place between the two markets.

At the same time, economic and financial policies have considerable implications for the exchange rate markets. At the macro level, the exchange markets do take into account the tendency of different currencies with regard to the competing currencies. For example, it has been contended that the euro was introduced to counter dollar influence and neutralize the effects of the dollar, especially on the European Union. At the same time, it has also been contended that the Chinese currency is also improving internationally, and demand for this currency is on the rise; this is mainly caused by the rise in the Chinese export, surplus budget, controlled unemployment rate, and inflation level, which are factors that directly and indirectly provide their effect on the international standing of Chinese currency.

The exchange rate and the stock market do not provide similar returns to their respective investors. Return has been defined as a profit that is expected by investors and shareholders from their investment in foreign currencies and shares of companies operational in different stock markets. In this regard, it is important to mention that return is a profit that is generated by the daily change taking place in foreign currencies and share prices as well. This change occurs in the market value of foreign currencies and stock prices. Sometimes, this change results in appreciation of currency and stock value, and sometimes decrease in price value is also observed by shareholders and investors.

The foreign exchange market is not fully as regulated as the stock market. Stock markets are placed at certain locations, such as the London Stock Exchange, and all other segments of this market are being operated inside this market. In order to control type of purchase, amount of shares, number of buying and selling of specific shares, there are certain regulatory requirements that are mostly complied with by the investors and shareholders. For example, the institutional shareholders will not be allowed to purchase all shares of one company in a single transaction, because this might create uncertainty in the market about the company and its relationship with the institutional shareholders. At the same time, there are certain stock-related regulations that are compulsorily followed by the investors and shareholders as well. On the other hand, the foreign currency exchange market is dispersed, and many small outlets are allowed to trade in foreign currencies. This spread of foreign currency markets makes it hard for the regulators and other monitoring bodies to effectively observe the buying and selling of foreign currencies. In other words, it is reasonable to elucidate that the foreign currency market is totally different when it comes to comparing it with the stock market because the latter is specifically located and is required to follow the regulatory guidelines of regulators.

Stock prices are mainly affected by three types of factors: economic factors, market factors, and firm factors (Madura 2008). Economic factors include minimum wage, trend in exports, employment and unemployment rates, inflation, interest rates, and so on. Market-related factors include overall investment climate and tendency of investors toward stock market growth and performance. Similarly, annual turnover, gross profit margin, net profit margin, net present value, dividend payout ratio, and strategic and operational policies of management for increasing return for shareholders are firm-related factors that directly affect stock prices.

Economic factors are directly related to the stock prices and their subsequent fluctuations. For example, an increase in minimum wage has direct negative consequence for firms because their profitability will be severely affected by this small change in minimum wage. More clearly, by increasing minimum wage from nine pounds to ten pounds, firms experience a rise in payroll, which will directly increase the cost of doing business, and this would decrease their profitability when the whole impact is considered on the business cost. This would also affect the shareholders and investors and they would try to avoid this cost through selling their shares which would result in decrease in share value. Additionally, market sentiment about particular stock or overall stock market performance is also highly relevant for ascertaining the influence of the factors on stock price fluctuations.

At the same time, stock prices are affected by the internal factors.

For example, it is expected that a firm's management will declare a very attractive returns and net profit; this positive sentiment and expectation will positively affect the stock price, and it will increase subsequently and vice versa. When compared with the factors affecting exchange rates, it can be easily deduced that as far as firm-related factors are concerned, they do not directly affect foreign exchange rate; in contrast, market factors and economic factors are directly associated with the foreign exchange rate because any substantial changes in these factors are also reflected by the change in the foreign exchange rate as well.

Existing Literature on the Relationship between Stock Market and Foreign Exchange Market Correlation

The recent literature provides a mixed picture over the relationship between stock market and exchange rate volatility. Bahmani-Oskooee and Sohrabian (1992) concludes bidirectional causality between stock price and exchange rate in the United Kingdom. Based on this point, it can be highlighted that not only are the effects of stock markets influencing the routine changes in foreign exchange rates, but also the fluctuations in the foreign exchange markets are visible in the stock markets. In other words, the London Stock Exchange and shares traded in it are being affected by the changes taking place in the foreign exchange rates inside the United Kingdom.

Koutoulas and Kryzanowski (1996) mention that there exists plausible evidence highlighting the positive relationship between stock market and exchange rate in Canada. In other words, it can be deduced that the decrease in the stock market also triggers decline in the foreign exchange rate. The US stock prices and exchange rates have carried out research and found the relationship between them (Roll 1992). Additionally, Kanas (2000) carried out empirical study for determining the relationship between the stock market and the exchange rate in the United States, Japan, Canada, the UK, and France; the subsequent results highlight that there exists a strong positive relationship between stock price and exchange rates. The same result has also been found by the study carried out to determine the relationship between stock prices and exchange rates in Japan (Wu 2005).

Research Aims and Objectives

The fundamental aim is to ascertain whether there exists any positive or negative correlation between following currencies on the indices and stock prices. Along with this objective, direction of any relationship will also be determined.

Research Objectives

1. To check that the test distribution is normal
2. To examine the causal relationship between the FTSE 100 index returns and six major currencies: GBP/USD, GBP/CHF, GBP/AUD, GBP/YEN, GBP/EURO, GBP/CAD
3. To understand the effect of exchange rate in terms of GBP/USD, GBP/CHF, GBP/AUD, GBP/YEN, GBP/EURO, and GBP/CAD on stock market returns at NASDAQ 100
4. To identify which exchange rates had positive and negative correlation to indices and stocks
5. To examine the causal relationship between the exchange rate of USD/CHF, EURO/USD, and AUD/USD and the FTSE 100 index returns
6. To check the effect of the exchange rate of USD/CHF, EURO/USD, and AUD/USD on the NASDAQ 100 returns
7. To open new vistas for further research

Hypotheses

H_{01}: Test distribution is normal.

H_{02}: There is no relationship between FTSE 100 index returns and foreign exchange rate of GBP/USD.

H_{03}: There is no relationship between FTSE 100 index returns and foreign exchange rate of GBP/CHF.

H_{04}: There is no relationship between FTSE 100 index returns and foreign exchange rate of GBP/AUD.

H_{05}: There is no relationship between FTSE 100 index returns and foreign exchange rate of GBP/YEN.

H_{06}: There is no relationship between FTSE 100 index returns and foreign exchange rate of GBP/EURO.

H_{07}: There is no relationship between FTSE 100 index returns and foreign exchange rate of GBP/CAD.

H_{08}: There is no effect of GBP/USD on NASDAQ 100 returns.

H_{09}: There is no effect of GBP/CHF on NASDAQ 100 returns.

H_{10}: There is no effect of GBP/AUD on NASDAQ 100 returns.

H_{11}: There is no effect of GBP/YEN on NASDAQ 100 returns.

H_{12}: There is no effect of GBP/EURO on NASDAQ 100 returns.

H_{13}: There is no effect of GBP/CAD on NASDAQ 100 returns.

H_{14}: There is no effect of exchange rate USD/CHF, EURO/USD, and AUD/USD on FTSE 100 index returns.

H_{15}: There is no effect of exchange rate USD/CHF, EURO/USD, and AUD/USD on NASDAQ 100 returns.

Research Methodology

Research Philosophy

Positivism and interpretivism are two main research philosophies for carrying out a research activity. Positivism refers to a research approach that uses scientific methods for conducting research. In this type of research methodology, scientific laws, rules, theories, and methods are used. This approach mainly relies on the use of numerical figures and numbers; in other words, the researcher will not be allowed to use his or her subjective understanding for deducing certain outcomes instead objective and natural laws are involved to determine and extract main findings.

The supporters of interpretivism use subjective understanding for evaluating and examining phenomena. In this type of research methodology, the researcher is empowered to use his or her own personal understanding for deriving certain outcomes; similarly, the researcher does not apply natural laws or numerical descriptions and signs for carrying out the work. As a result, it is reasonable to deduce that the theory of interpretivism is used when the theoretical foundations of positivism fail to satisfy certain research aims and objectives.

However, certain research objectives are not satisfied using only a single research philosophy; instead, they require the combined use and application of both research philosophies for obtaining the research objectives. Mixed methodology is a research methodology in which both positivism and interpretivism are used for deducing certain objectives. Keeping in view the research objectives of this approach, the researcher has used the mixed methodology by using both methodologies. For example, the literature review chapter is largely descriptive, critical, and theoretical. In this chapter, the researcher has included the previous research on the topic of interplay between stock market and the exchange rate market. In this part, the researcher has included theories such as monetarist model, asset market approach, classical economical theory, and research on the types of relationship between both factors. Subsequently, the researcher has critically evaluated them and tried to find out the gaps, themes, and weaknesses of certain models. In other words, it is reasonable to suggest that the work in this part is largely theoretical and descriptive, and the researcher is required to use inductive method for identifying patterns in the themes inbuilt to the previous research works of different authors. At the same time, the researcher is needed to interpret the relevant theories for assessing their relevance related to the research objectives. On the other hand, the work in the discussion and analysis chapter is largely based on the theory of positivism, where the numerical laws, natural theories, and scientific methods have been used to assess the level of relationship. In this regard, it is essential to highlight that the researcher has not used the subjective understanding for discussing and analyzing the tables mentioned in this chapter; instead, the tables are self-explanatory about the relationship between stock markets, share prices, and foreign exchange rates. As a result, it is essential and necessary to use the mixed research methodology for satisfying the research objectives.

Data Collection Method

Secondary research has been mainly used for collecting the relevant data and information from different sources. Fundamentally, there are two methods employed for collecting data: a primary method and a secondary method. In the primary data collection method, a researcher is required to access the firsthand information from the potential respondents, whereas in secondary research the researcher uses preexisting data and information for obtaining the research objectives. In this regard, it is important to mention that the primary research method is considered to be more effective when it is compared with the secondary research data collection method, because the former gives access to the firsthand information or data. However, it is still pertinent to highlight that the secondary data collection method is mainly relevant for this paper for obtaining the research objectives. First, the scope of the research aim and objectives is considerably wide and common. This is mainly caused by the fact that the relationship between the stock markets, share prices, and exchange rates is considerably international, and it cannot be ascertained or assessed through collecting one hundred or three hundred respondents from both industries. At the same time, it is also relevant to highlight that the exchange rates are not specific to any particular country; more clearly, the exchange rates are international in their very nature, and they have been used for assessing their relationship with certain stock prices and stock markets.

For obtaining the research objectives, the researcher has used two websites: Yahoo finance and Oanda.com. From these sources, observations relating to the FTSE 100 index and the NASDAQ 100 index and exchange rates of different currencies have been taken from the start of 2012 to the end of 2014.

Data Analysis Method

The variable samples were tested with the normality of the data series using PASW 18. The basic assumption for forming a regression model is that the data distribution should be normal. Further, the two variables and their relationship have been mainly assessed through the use of Excel 2007 and PASW 18. The independent variable and dependent variables have been used for evaluating the relationship between the stock markets, share prices, and exchange rate for the course of three years. Here, the independent variable is x, and y is a dependent variable. In this regard, it is pertinent to highlight that the FTSE 100 index and NASDAQ 100 index have been used independent variables, whereas the exchange rates have been mostly used as dependent variables. However, in order to ascertain the casualty effect, a few exchange rates have been as independent variables.

Subsequently, there are thirty-six observations in each table mention in the discussion and analysis chapter, where twelve observations have been taken from January 2012 to the end of December 2014. After collecting the data, the researcher has used the regression model, developed in the MS Excel 2007 and PASW 18, for evaluating the correlation of different independent and dependent variables. After applying the regression model, the obtained results have been depicted through the regression tables mentioned in the chapter on discussion and analysis.

Additionally, the researcher has used an effective discussion and analysis strategy. First, the researcher has explained the type of relationship. After establishing the relationship, the relevant points from the literature review have been used to further discuss and analyze the relationship. In this regard, it is important to highlight that the researcher has mainly discussed the relationship after ascertaining strength of relationship between the variables.

Validity and Reliability

Validity is mostly concerned with data in contrast to reliability, which is more related to the data source. The use of valid data is of crucial importance for any research activity because it provides confidence to all who are interested to read and understand any research work. Keeping this view in mind, the researcher has used only valid data. For example, the researcher has used the numerical information about the variables involved for obtaining the research objectives of this paper. Similarly, the use and importance of reliability is of pivotal significance for any research activity because it represents data integrity. In order to satisfy this aspect, the researcher has used the official and authentic sources for collecting the relevant data—for example, Yahoo finance, which is a authentic and reputable source for providing information relating to the FTSE 100 index and NASDAQ 100 index. Additionally, the official website of Oanda.com is a Canada-based foreign exchange rate agency, providing data relating to foreign exchange rates of all currencies and their historical performance and changes taking place in their relationship.

Research Ethics

The researcher has not used others' ideas and their perspectives in the paper. Plagiarism has become a serious academic offence. Therefore in order to avoid this serious academic issue, the researcher has not used ideas of other authors without giving them due credit. For example, the researcher has fully referenced them by mentioning their name and year for in-text citations, as well as reference list. At the same time, it is also unethical to ask for support from friends, colleagues, and teachers. In order to avoid this problem, the researcher has not relied on the support of any friends; instead, all work has been done without the support of anyone. This is important because this is purely individual work, and it must not be tampered with by others.

Results and Analysis

Regression Analysis

It is a linear regression model, which is determined by the procedure of minimizing the squares of errors. It is represented as a linear line, where the space between the regression line and each observation is lessened. It is executed to know the cause and effect relationship between the two variables in the study. One of them is the dependent variable and the other is the explanatory variable, where it explains the behavior of the dependent variable. The selection of the variables depends on the objectives of the study, which is simplified in the hypothesis.

In the present context, the researcher aims to check the existence of the causal relationship between the variables—namely, exchange rate against GBP and stock returns in NASDAQ 100 and FTSE 100. Here, the dependent variable is stock returns, which as explained by the exchange rates is the aim of the study.

For this purpose, the following regression model is framed as:

$$Y = a + bx + \varepsilon$$

Where
Y = dependent variable (stock returns)
X = independent variable (exchange rate)
a = intercept of regression line
b = slope of regression line
ε = error term

The model is the expression of the causal relationship between Y (here, stock returns), which is dependent on X (here, exchange rate). The b is the slope of the regression line, usually called beta, which explains the unit changes in dependent variable for every unit change in independent variable. Suppose $b = 0.73$. That would signify if the independent variable changes with a certain amount, then the dependent variable will also change with 0.73 times that amount. Further, the intercept (a/alpha) indicates the value of the dependent variable when the independent is zero.

In investment parlance, a manager has a positive alpha because a linear regression between the manager's performance and the performance of the market has an intercept number greater than 0.

Normality of the Data Distribution

Table 1: Normality Statistics

		USD	CHF	AUD	YEN	EURO	CAD	FTSE	NASDAQ
N		31	31	31	31	31	31	31	31
Normal Parameters[a,b]	Mean	1.6020	1.4807	1.6368	148.3123	1.2144	1.6547	3.8033	3.4799
	Std. Deviation	.05357	.03461	.14176	20.65179	.03453	.10770	.02900	.07126
Most Extreme Differences	Absolute	.099	.105	.217	.162	.122	.284	.195	.179
	Positive	.099	.105	.217	.162	.101	.284	.135	.179
	Negative	-.066	-.084	-.159	-.136	-.122	-.154	-.195	-.109
Kolmogorov-Smirnov Z		.553	.586	1.209	.903	.681	1.579	1.088	.994
Asymp. Sig. (2-tailed)		.919	.882	.107	.388	.743	.124	.187	.276

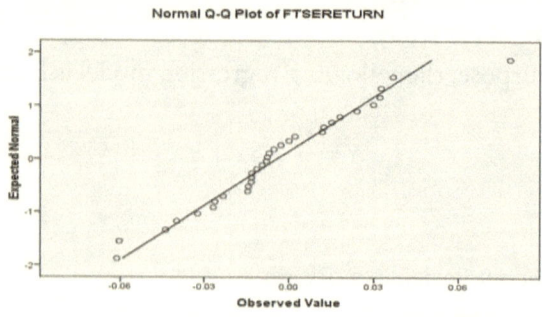

Normal Q-Q Plot of FTSERETURN

One of the assumptions of the linear regression model is normality of the data; it explains that the distribution of error terms is normal. The data used for the regression analysis was tested with the KS normality tests, where the results were found to be normal, because the KS statistics are insignificant (i.e., more than 5 percent level of significance). This helps in accepting the null hypothesis, which says that the test distribution is normal.

Data of exchange rate of GBP against USD is normally distributed because it is insignificant at a 91 percent level of significance, implying the null hypothesis is not rejected. Also, the exchange rate of GBP/USD, GBP/CHF, GBP/AUD, GBP/YEN, GBP/EURO, and GBP/CAD is insignificant at 88.2 percent, 10.7 percent, 38.8 percent, 74.3 percent, 12.4 percent, 18.7 percent, and 27.6 percent, respectively.

Table 2: Regression Statistics between Financial Times Stock Exchange
(FTSE) and Exchange Rate in Great Britain Pound (GBP)

S. No.	Variables	R^2	F-Value	Sig.	T-Value	Sig.	Beta
1.	FTSE and GBP/US	0.252	10.11	0.003	3.18	0.003	0.502
2.	FTSE and GBP/CHF	0.14	5.51	0.025	-0.23	0.025	-0.374
3.	FTSE and GBP/AUD	0.77	99.25	0.00	-9.96	0.00	-0.88
4.	FTSE and GBP/Yen	0.77	101.27	0.00	-10.06	0.00	-0.88
5.	FTSE and GBP/Euro	0.11	4.14	0.50	-2.03	0.05	-0.33
6.	FTSE and GBP/CAD	0.865	185.5	0.00	-13.62	0.00	-0.930

The results were estimated for determining the causal relationship between the dependent variable, which is FTSE returns, and the exchange rate against six major currencies, which is the independent variable. The relationship was established by testing the regression model as shown below.

$$Y = a + b(x) + e$$

FTSE returns = .281 + 3.351 (GBP/USD) + e

For this model, the assessment period has been taken from January 2012 to December 2014, a total of three years. In this graph, two variables, FTSE 100 index and GBP/US exchange rate, have been used. In order to determine the relationship between these two variables, the FTSE 100 index has been used as an independent variable, whereas the GBP/US exchange rate has been used as a dependent variable. Subsequently, the strength of relationship is determined through knowing the R-squared value between -1 and +1; the relationship is said to be stronger and positive when R-squared is near to +1 or more than 0.5 level, and the negative or no relationship exists when the R-squared falls near to -1 or less than -0.5 level.

The results explained that the R^2 value is 25 percent, which implies that only 25 percent variance is caused by GBP/USD in FTSE 100 index returns. This is due to a flow of funds that is not majorly in US dollars. The t-statistics are 3.18, which is significant at 0 percent level of significance, indicating the existence of the causal relationship (i.e., exchange rate of USD impacts the returns at FTSE). This helps in rejecting H_{02}, explaining the GBP/USD affects the returns at FTSE 100 index returns. Also, the model was tested with the fitness, which is found to be fit, because the F-value is significant at 0 percent level of significance.

This finding is supported with the results of Aggarwal (1991), where the results were found to be positive with regard to the relationship between the GBP/USD and FTSE 100 index returns. Additionally, it is also pertinent to highlight that economic factors are those factors that directly or indirectly affect changes in the exchange rates. At the same time, this finding also proves that there is a linear relationship between two variables. However, in this regard, it is important to mention that correlation between FTSE 100 index and GBP/US exchange rate has an R-squared of 25 percent, as mentioned in the table 2. In other words, only a 25 percent change in FTSE 100 index can be reflected by GBP/US exchange rate value during the period of last three years.

Moreover, there are certain reasons that might be appropriate to evaluate the presence of a relationship, but not a strong relationship, between these two factors. First, the pound and the dollar reflect two stable, strong economies of the trade world, where regulators and economic and financial indicators largely remain stable, and there remains little room for any abnormal changes in these economies. Because exchange rates largely reflect the economic outlook of their economies, the effect of related economic and financial policies can also be found in the stable variation in the exchange rates. The same has been reflected by the weak relationship between FTSE 100 index and the GBP/US exchange rate.

Also, it was found that changing the position of variables does not change much in the subsequent results. For example, when the FTSE 100 index is used as an independent and as a dependent variable, the subsequent outcome did not change, equally demonstrating that the R-squared remains the same, showing little relationship between FTSE and GBP/US exchange rate. The FTSE 100 index is a highly regulated sector, whereas the GBP/US exchange rate is not regulated as much because the latter's market is scattered, and little changes for controlling and regulating it similar to the FTSE 100 index regulation. Moreover, this finding has also been highlighted in the literature review chapter as well. Solnik (1978) insists that there effects or changes in exchange rates are not reflected by the stock markets.

Phylaktis and Ravazzolo (2005) reflect that flow-oriented model assumes that the effects to currency changes directly affects the international trade balance and real output of an economy, which subsequently affects the firm's cash flows and their share prices as well. However, this perspective has been found.

Further, the relationship was also tested by taking another largest traded currency, the Swiss franc, in terms of Britain sterling (GBP) with FTSE 100 index returns from January 2012 to December 2014. The following regression model was used.

$$\textbf{FTSE returns} = \textbf{4.295} + \textbf{(-0.335)} \ \textbf{(GBP/CHF)} + \textbf{e}$$

When the above model was applied, the R^2 value came out to be 14 percent, explaining that Swiss franc is causing only 14 percent variance in the dependent variable. Here, the Swiss franc is explaining the FTSE 100 index returns by only 14 percent. Additionally, this proves that any variation in FTSE 100 index has not been reflected by the GBP/CHF exchange rate during the reported period. In this regard, it is significant to mention that this finding also disapproves the validity of classical economic theory, which is based on the assumption that there exists a relationship between stock market and foreign exchange rate, because in the present case the R-squared value is too low. Moreover, it has been argued that in the fully integrated financial markets, exchange rate variation is also reflected by the stock prices (Zapatero 1995). However, this perspective has been unfound in the above table, in which R-squared is 14 percent, demonstrating no relationship between these factors. The t-statistics revealed the existence of the causal relationship between the Swiss franc and FTSE 100 index returns. When supported with the R-squared results, it can be said that there is a relationship, but a weak one. Therefore H_{03} was rejected, implying the existence of the causal relationship. Also, the model fitness was checked, which was again found to be low with a 5.51 value with a 2.5 percent level of significance.

When the exchange rate of the Australian dollar (AUD) against the GBP was regressed with FTSE 100 index returns, the following model was formulated.

$$\text{FTSE returns} = 4.098 + (-0.180)\,(\text{AUD}) + e$$

This table reflects a strong, positive relationship between the FTSE 100 index and the GBP/AUD exchange rate. The above table reflects R-squared is 75 percent, clearly demonstrating that 75 percent variation can also be reflected by the changes in the GBP/AUD exchange rate, especially from January 2012 to December 2014.

This finding proves both the first and second hypotheses. In the first hypothesis, it has been assumed that there exists a relationship between the stock market and the foreign exchange market. When this assumption is applied to ascertaining the relationship between FTSE 100 index and the foreign exchange rate of the GBP/AUD, the subsequent result shows 75 percent R-squared, proving the relationship between the FTSE 100 index and the GBP/AUD exchange rate from 2012 to 2014. Additionally, it is appropriate to mention that the correlation between the FTSE 100 index and the GBP/AUD exchange rate is not only positive but also strong, because the strength of relationship, which is reflected by the R-squared (i.e., 75 percent), remains more close to +1. That is a sign of a strong relationship between the independent variable and the dependent variable. Also, t-statistics approved this relationship with a value of -9.963 with a 0 percent level of significance. That makes the relationship stronger and rejects H_{04}. The model was also found to be highly fit, with an F-value of 99.25 with a 0 percent level of significance.

This finding also validates and disapproves certain models. For example, the monetarist model indicates that there exists a relationship between the stock market and exchange markets (Gavin 1989). This model is clearly proven by this finding because the stock market (FTSE 100 index) has found a positive and strong relationship with the foreign exchange rate (GBP/AUD), showing that the model is not only theoretically understandable but also practically provable. At the same time, it is pertinent to mention that this model also assumes the causality effect first takes place in the stock market, and subsequently it affects the changes in the exchange rate (Gavin 1989). In other words, it can be deduced that the same has also been proven by this finding because the 75 percent variation in the FTSE 100 index can also be reflected by the changes in the GBP/AUD exchange rate.

On the other hand, this finding does not prove the validity of the asset market approach model. Dornbusch and Fisher (1980) contend that the asset market approach is based on the assumption that the causality effect first occurs in the exchange rate, and subsequently the stock market is affected by this change. In other words, changes in the stock market do not first take place and affect the exchange rate; instead, changes in the foreign exchange rate are the first to appear, and then they impact the variation in the stock markets. When this is applied to the current finding, it can be easily extracted that this model's assumptions are unfound because changes in the stock market (FTSE 100 index) have directly impacted the changes in the exchange rate (GBP/AUD) from the period of January 2012 to December 2014.

The regression model was framed, taking into consideration the Japanese Yen with GBP and FTSE 100 index returns.

$$\text{FTSE returns} = 3.987 + (-.001)\,(\text{GBP/YEN}) + e$$

The relationship between FTSE 100 index and the GBP/Yen exchange rate is both positive and strong as well. The above table exhibits an R-squared of 77 percent, showing the strength of the relationship between both variables during the period. This indicates that 77 percent variation in the FTSE 100 index can also be reflected by the GBP/Yen exchange rate during the reported period. It proves the hypothesis that the stock market and exchange rate are highly correlated. The t-statistics explain the existence of the strong but negative relationship between the FTSE 100 index returns and GBP/YEN. The t-value, which was -10.064, had a 0 percent level of significance, rejecting $H_{05.}$ It is also observed that the model has a high fit, with an F-value of 101.27 with a 0 percent level of significance.

This finding is closely in line with some theoretical models and previous research carried out on the relationship between the stock market and the exchange rate. Aggarwal (1981) finds a plausible relationship between the stock market and the exchange rate. Similarly, the monetarist model and classical economic theory have similar perspectives on the relationship between these two variables. However, it is still pertinent to highlight that some authors have different perspectives on this issue. For example, it has been contended that bidirectional causality exists between stock price and exchange rate in the United Kingdom (Bahmani-Osokee and Sohrabian 1992). Their perspective is also reflected by this finding because the FTSE 100 index and the GBP/Yen exchange rate have shown a strong, positive relationship. This point is valid when evaluating the relationship between an independent variable and a dependent variable. In this case, the FTSE 100 index has been used as an independent variable, whereas the GBP/Yen exchange rate was a dependent variable.

Another set of causal relationship has been established between the exchange rate EURO/GBP and FTSE 100 index returns. The following regression model was used.

$$\text{FTSE returns} = 4.154 + (-0.292)\,(\text{GBP/EURO}) + e$$

The results shown in table 2 explained that R-squared value was too low to cause a variance in the dependent variable (i.e., FTSE returns from 2012 to the end of 2014). It was found to be only 10.9 percent of variance caused in the index returns at FTSE. This meant that the euro was not playing a significant role in determining the FTSE 100. Further, the t-statistics was found was to have a 5 percent level of significance with -2.035. It should be noted that model was found to low fit when the F-value of 4.142 revealed a 5 percent level of significance. The model was also tested with the outliers, and no outliers were identified in this relationship; therefore the degree of freedom remained 34 items. The null hypothesis H_{06} was rejected, implying the existing of a causal relationship between the sample variables in the study.

At the same time, it is interesting to note that the values do not show any relationship between the FTSE 100 index and the GBP/US exchange rate; the same is also reflected in this case, with same period as well. In this regard, it is pertinent to deduce that the exchange rate of two stable economies does not retain any relationship with the stock markets. This point is also proven by the GBP/USD relationship with the FTSE 100 index returns.

The relationship was tested by taking the exchange rate of the Canadian dollar with the GBP and FTSE 100 index returns. The following model was developed.

$$\textbf{FTSE returns} = \textbf{4.218} + \textbf{(-0.250) (GBP/CAD)} + \textbf{e}$$

The results depicted in the above table show a strong, positive relationship between the FTSE 100 index and the GBP/CAD exchange rate. The R-squared is 0.865, which indicated that the 86 percent variation in the FTSE 100 index is reflected by the changes in the GBP/CAD exchange rate during the period from 2012 to 2014.

This finding proves the first two hypotheses by showing the highest R-squared between the two variables. The FTSE 100 index represents 100 companies that are registered in the London Stock Exchange, and the registered companies are both national and international. In other words, the companies, which are being reflected by the FTSE 100 index, are not only reflecting the performance of national companies but also demonstrating the stocks of international firms, operating in more than one country. In this regard, it is relevant to highlight that this finding also proves international competitiveness and international trade (which mostly reflects the international currencies) have a positive relationship with the stocks and cash flows of these companies. More important, this finding is not restricted to the United Kingdom, where the FTSE 100 index and the GBP/CAD exchange rate retain a strong and positive relationship. It is also found in Canada as well (Koutoulas and Kryzanowski 1996). At the same time, the relationship was found to be strong with a t-value of -13.62 and a 0 percent level of significance. This explains that the null hypothesis was rejected, which implies the existence of a strong, negative relationship. Also, the model was found to be highly fit with an F-value 185.53 and a 0 percent level of significance. This helps in rejecting H_{07}. The reasons for this kind of relationship are the increasing investments by Canadians in the FTSE and the improving trade of the FOREX of Canada.

Table 3: Regression Statistics between NASDAQ 100 and Exchange Rate in Great Britain Pound (GBP)

S. No.	Variables	R^2	F-Value	Sig.	T-Value	Sig.	Beta
1.	NASDAQ and GBP/US	0.175	7.20	0.01	-2.684	.0.01	-0.418
2.	NASDAQ and GBP/CHF	0.092	3.46	0.07	1.86	0.07	0.304
3.	NASDAQ and GBP/AUD	0.876	240.70	0.00	15.51	0.00	0.93
4.	NASDAQ and GBP/Yen	0.906	326.53	0.00	18.07	0.00	0.952
5.	NASDAQ and GBP/Euro	0.12	4.43	0.043	2.11	0.04	0.34
6.	NASDAQ and GBP/CAD	0.83	164.00	0.00	12.89	0.00	0.91

The regression models were also framed for testing the causal relationship between the NASDAQ returns and six major currencies: GBP/USD, GBP/CHF, GBP/AUD, GBP/YEN, GBP/EURO, and GBP/CAD. This was done in order to validate the existence of the effect of exchange rates on the NASDAQ stock market. The first model of regression can be seen as follows.

NASDAQ returns = 4.471 + (-0.612) (GBP/USD) + e

This model explains the causal relationship between the NASDAQ 100 and the exchange rate of GBP/USD. The results revealed that the R-squared is 16 percent, which shows that the variables have no relationship because R-squared is considerably lower. In this regard, it is important to mention that the NASDAQ 100 index is a US-based stock market, and the international foreign exchange rate of GBP/US has been used to evaluate the correlation. This result has disapproved the first hypothesis. This disapproval clearly highlights that all stock markets are not correlated with foreign exchange rates, as reflected in some of the earlier tables. Moreover, this finding is also in line with the earlier work of other researchers on this topic. For example, Franck and Young (1972) reflect that there exists no relationship between stock markets and foreign exchange rate. However, moderate relationship between US stock prices and the US dollar exchange rate has been found from the period of 1971 to the end of 1987 (Jorion 1990).

Because the R-squared value is too low even though the relationship is there (as t-statistics are significant at a 5 percent level of significance), it is assumed that the relationship does not exists. The fitness of the model was tested by computing the F-value, which had a 0.01 percent level of significance. This rejects H_{08} and implies that model was low fit with a low value, which was 7.202. It was tested with outliers, and none were found—hence the degree of freedom remained at 34 items.

The model was framed to test the relationship between the Swiss franc with the GBP and NASDAQ returns. It was as follows.

NASDAQ returns = 2.540 + 0.642 (GBP/CHF) + e

This model also revealed the low causal relationship. This was enumerated by the R-squared value, which was too low to cause a variance in the dependent variable (NASDAQ 100 returns). This means that Swiss franc is influencing the returns at NASDAQ by only 9 percent. Furthermore, because of the financial crises in Switzerland, the currency of the country is facing overvaluation. It was seen that the Swizz market was hit hard by commercial banks' lending policies, which were associated with fixing the exchange rate with the euro. Even the lowering of the interest rates caused the economy to be in deflationary pressures, in lieu of improvements in the purchasing power of the population. Therefore, this did not influence the US stock market much (Source: http://www. nasdaq.com/article/swiss-national-bank-policy-and-its-implications-for -currencies-assets-and-central-banking-cm441483). Further, the relationship was found to be a positive one, where the t-value was found to have a 10 percent level of significance. This also helps in rejecting H_{09}. Therefore, it can be said that causal relationship existed running from GBP/CHF toward NASDAQ 100 returns, but those were found to be very low or negligible. It can be concluded that the Swiss franc is unable to influence the NASDAQ returns; therefore, investors' decisions toward investing in the Swiss franc would not impact their investments in NASDAQ.

Another set of relationship was established between GBP/AUD and NASDAQ 100 returns, which can be demonstrated as follows.

NASDAQ returns = 2.683 + 0.488 (GBP/AUD) + e

Table 13 demonstrates both a positive and strong relationship between the NASDAQ 100 index and the GBP/AUD exchange rate. The observations have been taken from the period 2012 to the end of 2014; the NASDAQ 100 index has been used as an independent variable, whereas the R-squared has been taken as a dependent variable. Subsequently, the result demonstrates that the R-squared is 87.6 percent, which demonstrates that the NASDAQ 100 index retains a positive and strong relationship with the GBP/AUD exchange rate during the reported period. Furthermore, the relationship was made strong by the t-value, which had a 5 percent level of significance, indicating that 15.515 times the relationship was impacted by the trade in AUD at NASDAQ stock exchange. Here, it can be said that H_{10} is rejected. Moreover, the model was found to be highly fit with an F-value of 240.70 at 0 percent significance.

This finding also proves the validity of previous research on this topic. Roll (1992) investigated the relationship between stock market and exchange rates, and the results highlighted a strong relationship between these two variables. Kana (2000) conducted a study for ascertaining the relationship between the stock market and the exchange rate in the United States; the subsequent results highlighted that both variables retained a positive and strong correlation during the analysis period. This proves that this relationship between the stock market and the exchange rates has largely been found in the United States, because the existing study has proven the validity of this claim as well.

The following regression model was framed for evaluating the causality relationship between the NASDAQ returns and GBP/YEN.

NASDAQ returns = 2.969 + 0.003 (GBP/YEN) + e

The results display a strong, positive relationship between the NASDAQ 100 index and the GBP/Yen exchange rate. The R-squared is 90.6 percent, showing the highest level of strength between the two variables. This is the most interesting finding for a number of reasons. The relationship was expressed with a t-value being 18.07 significant at 0 percent. Therefore, H_{11} is rejected. Also, the model was highly fit with an F-value of 326.53 with 0 percent significant value, rejecting the null hypothesis H_{11}. As a result, this proves that internationally the exchange rate of the GBP/Yen has retained both the positive and strong relationship between two separately located stock markets (i.e., the FTSE 100 index and the NASDAQ 100 index); one is located in the United Kingdom, and the other is situated in the United States. At the same time, they do not operate in a similar economic, political, and financial environment, but each has its own economic, political, and financial factors that directly and indirectly affect the changes in the stock markets and the exchange rates.

This table does not depict any relationship between the two variables in the reported period. This finding reflects the observations taken from the period of 2012 to 2014, where the NASDAQ 100 index has been utilized as an independent variable and the GBP/EURO exchange rate has been used to represent a dependent variable. This finding is totally in line to the perspectives given in the literature review. Frankel (1983) reflects that the asset market approach is based on the premise that the stock prices directly affect the exchange rates.

However, when this perspective is applied to the current study, the findings reveal that the NASDAQ 100 index has no relationship with the GBP/EURO exchange rate during the period from 2012 to 2014, demonstrating that the asset market approach has not been empirically proven by the findings provided by the results in the table.

The regression model formulated is seen as:

NASDAQ returns = 2.629 + 0.709 (GBP/EURO) + e

The R-squared value in this model is 0.115, explaining that only 11.5 percent variance is caused by GBP/EURO in the US stock market (i.e., NASDAQ 100). However, t-stats reveal the existence of a positive relationship with 4.3 percent significance level. Therefore, H_{12} is rejected. Also, the model was tested with the fitness, which was also found to be low with an F-value of 4.430, significant at 4.3 percent.

The regression model for NASDAQ 100 returns and GBP/CAD was tested as follows.:

NASDAQ returns = 2.476 + 0.608 (GBP/CAD) + e

This table shows an R-squared of 83 percent between the NASDAQ 100 index and the GBP/CAD exchange rate. The observations have been taken from January 2012 to December 2014. In this attempt, the NASDAQ 100 index has been used as an independent variable, and the GBP/CAD was a dependent variable. The subsequent result denotes that 83 percent of changes in the NASDAQ 100 index can also be explained by the changes in the GBP/CAD exchange rate during the reported period. This finding considerably substantiates previous related theoretical underpinnings and previous research on the interplay between the stock market and the exchange rate. Phylaktis and Ravazzolo (2005) elucidate that the classical economic theory is based on the premise that stock markets and exchange rates always retain positive correlation. Moreover, it has also been mentioned that association between stock price and exchange rate is mainly caused by the full integration of financial markets (Zapatero 1995). Consequently, if this perspective is applied to the relationship between the NASDAQ 100 index and the GBP/CAD exchange rate, the subsequent results substantiate the notion of Zapatero and classical economic theory. Similarly, the previous research on this topic authenticates the perspectives of these authors. For example, the US stock prices retain positive correlation with the exchange rates; this has been found empirically (Roll 1992; Kanas 2000). Hence, null hypothesis H_{13} is rejected.

Based on this finding, it can be easily deduced that the changes in the exchange rate between the GBP/CAD can easily be influenced by the changes affecting and taking place in the NASDAQ 100 index, because this relationship has retained both a positive and strong tendency with each other.

Table 4: Regression Statistics between Financial Times Stock Exchange (FTSE) and Exchange Rate in USD

S. No.	Variables	R^2	F-Value	Sig.	T-Value	Sig.	Beta
1.	FTSE and Euro/USD	0.13	5.196	0.02	-2.2795	0.029	1.533
2.	FTSE and USD/CHF	0.15	6.24	0.017	2.498	0.017	0.782
3.	FTSE and AUD/USD	0.58	47.03	6.77E-08	6.85	6.77E-08	0.24
4.	NASDAQ and Euro/USD	0.05	1.822	0.18	1.34	0.18	1.25
5.	NASDAQ and USD/CHF	0.05	2.011	0.16	-1.418	0.16	0.96
6.	NASDAQ and AUD/USD	0.76	113.02	2.38E-12	10.63	2.38E-12	1.3

The above table exhibits no relationship between the FTSE 100 index and the Euro/USD exchange rate. In this table, R-squared is 13 percent, showing only a 13 percent change in the FTSE that can be reflected by the change in the Euro/USD exchange rate from 2012 to the end of 2014. This finding is the most interesting and of crucial importance. When compared with table 1, where the GBP as the primary currency exchange with other currencies has been used, it provides different perspectives on the correlation between the national currency and international currencies. For example, in table 1, there is a positive and strong relationship between the FTSE 100 index and the exchange rates of other currencies relating to the GBP. More clearly, the strength of their relationship is considerably higher, reaching a level of 86 percent maximum and 75 percent minimum during the reported period. Based on this situation, it is reasonable to deduce that the variations in the FTSE 100 index have a close resemblance with the variations taking place in the GBP exchange rates with other currencies. On the other hand, when the FTSE 100 index, used as an independent variable, is analyzed with other currencies, the relationship is mostly unfound.

Table 2 exhibits no interplay between the FTSE 100 index and the USD/CHF exchange rate. The table highlights 15 percent R-squared, which is insufficient to prove any relationship between the FTSE 100 index and the USD/CHF exchange rate during the period of 2012 to 2014.

One can deduce certain reasons for this finding. First, the FTSE 100 index is located in the United Kingdom, whereas the USD and CHF are national currencies of the United States of America and Switzerland, respectively. In the literature review, it is clearly stipulated that the frequency of transactions in the foreign exchange currencies largely remains fewer, whereas frequency of transactions in the stock markets is higher and more frequent. Because both currencies are international and are not mostly traded in other countries, such as the United Kingdom. Therefore it is reasonable to expect no relationship between the FTSE 100 index and the USD/CHF exchange rate. However, it is still pertinent to highlight that at the international level, these currencies may be more frequent and might be in great demand, but even that does not prove any relationship with the FTSE 100 index.

Table 3 shows a positive relationship between the FTSE 100 index and the AUD/USD exchange rate during the reported period. The table reflects the R-squared which is 58 percent, showing that 58 percent variation in the FTSE 100 index can be explained by the movements in the AUD/USD exchange rate from 2012 to 2014. In all the cases, the null hypothesis H_{14} is rejected, explaining the existence of the relationship between the variables.

Table 3 also shows no relationship between both variables. The NASDAQ 100 index and the EURO/USD exchange rate have been used as an independent and a dependent variable, respectively. For assessing the strength of their relationship, three years' performance has been selected and used. The subsequent result reveals that the R-squared is 5 percent, clearly demonstrating that only 5 percent variation in the NASDAQ 100 index can also be explained by the changes in the EURO/USD exchange rate during the reported period. This highlights that both variables have failed to prove the validity of first two hypotheses during the reported period. The null hypothesis was rejected because two exchange rates do not impact NASDAQ returns.

In the previous research on this topic, findings have been mixed. Some results indicate the presence of both positive and strong relationship between stock markets and exchange rates, whereas others point out absence of relationship between these variables. For example, Solnik (1987) carried out research on this topic and found no correlation between the share prices and exchange rates during the evaluation period.

It also provides no relationship between the variables during the analyzed period. This is the most important finding for various reasons. The independent variable (NASDAQ 100 index) is situated in the United States, and the exchange rate is the US dollar with the Swiss franc. In other words, the dollar exchange rate is considerably related to the NASDAQ because they both reflect the exchange market and stock market in the United States. Based on this finding, it can be deduced that it is not necessary that the stock market and exchange rate of the same country irrelevant or need to be interlinked. Instead, different factors influence different exchanges rates, and it is not necessary that they both the exchange rate and the stock market be related to the same economy. In other words, a positive correlation between the stock market and the exchange rate cannot be established simply because of their relevance to the same country.

It also shows a relationship between the NASDAQ 100 index and the AUD/USD exchange rate. The R-squared shows the relationship strength of 76 percent, reflecting both a positive and strong relationship between the NASDAQ 100 index and the AUD/USD exchange rate.

This finding proves that even an international currency exchange rate can be closely associated with an international stock market. For example, NASDAQ is a US-based stock market where shares of local and international firms are routinely traded. In contrast, the AUD/USD exchange rate represents the exchange rate of the Australian dollar with regard to the US dollar. Their positive and strong correlation clearly demonstrates that the stock market of one country can have a relationship with the exchange rate of another country's currency. Based on this situation, it is reasonable to deduce that the global economy, financial markets, and stock markets are highly integrated, and it is the result of this integration and interlink that create correlation even between two geographically located economies, exchange rates, and stock markets. At the same time, export between two economies, demand for foreign currency, and resemblance in economic and financial policies are factors that directly and indirectly affect the correlation between the variables working within the same system.

Conclusion

The purpose was to ascertain the relationship between the stock markets and the exchange rates. This paper has attempted to address the basic objective of the study: examining the cause and effect relationship between the variables. This included different stock markets (FTSE 100 and NASDAQ 100) and exchange rates that have been regressed for ascertaining the type of relationship between these variables. For this purpose, the period from 2012 to 2014 was chosen, and each variable was individually regressed against other variable.

Overall, the research findings are mixed. Some variables have both positive and strong relationships, whereas others have no relationship. First, the FTSE 100 index, which was mainly used as an independent variable, has not maintained a uniform relationship with the exchange rates of different currencies. It is interesting to find that the FTSE 100 index has no relationship with the GBP/US exchange rate despite the fact that the FTSE 100 index and the GBP are both related to the United Kingdom, because the former is a main and important stock market, and the latter is the national currency of the country. At the same time, it is interesting to highlight that in table 1, the FTSE 100 index has been used as an independent variable, and the GBP/US exchange rate has been utilized as a dependent variable. Similarly, the GBP/CHF exchange rate as an independent variable and the FTSE 100 index as a dependent variable shows the same result, as is demonstrated by table 1. Interestingly, table 1, where the FTSE 100 index and the GBP/AUD exchange rate have been regressed, shows a positive and strong relationship between the variables: the R-squared is 77 percent from the start of 2012 to the end of 2014. Similarly, it also shows an R-squared of 77 percent between the FTSE 100 index and the GBP/

Yen during the reported period. When considering the FTSE 100 index as an independent variable, the result shows that the FTSE 100 index has been used a total of nine times with the different exchange rates, which have been used as dependent variables during the reported period. Out of nine times, the FTSE 100 index has been able to develop mostly positive and strong relationship with four exchange rates (GBP/AUD, GBP/Yen, GBP/CAD, and AUD/USD). On the other hand, the FTSE 100 index has not maintained any relationship with the following foreign exchange rates: the GBP/US exchange rate, the GBP/CHF exchange rate, the GBP/EURO exchange rate, the EURO/USD exchange rate, and the USD/CHF exchange rate. Based on this situation, it can be deduced that the FTSE 100 index has not maintained a positive and strong relationship with the majority of the exchange rates, as reflected in the respective tables. It was found that relationship existed but was near negligible because of low R-squared values in the case of GBP/USD, GBP/CHF, and GBP/EURO.

The same situation is also depicted when the NASDAQ 100 index has been used as an independent variable and has been regressed with the different exchange rates during the reported period of time. Overall, the NASDAQ 100 index has been observed and analyzed with nine different exchange rates, and this independent variable has only maintained three strong relationships with the dependent variables; no relationship has been found with three variables.

It can be deduced that the relationship where it was found, as well as the economic factors, play an important role in affecting FTSE 100 and NASDAQ 100 returns. This can help in giving direction to further research for analyzing the factors determining exchange rates and such stock indices.

References

Aggarwal, R. 1981. "Exchange Rates and Stock Prices: A Study of the US Capital Markets under Floating Exchange Rates." *Akron Business and Economic Review* (Fall): 7–12.

Dornbusch, R., and S. Fisher. 1980. "Exchange Rates and the Current Account." *American Economic Review* 70: 960–971.

Frankel, J. A. 1983. "Monetary and Portfolio Balance Models of Exchange Rate Determination." In *Economic Interdependence and Flexible Exchange Rates*, edited by J. S. Bhandari and B. H. Putnam. Cambridge: MIT Press.

Gavin, M. 1989. "The Stock Market and Exchange Rate Dynamics." *Journal of International Money and Finance* 8: 181–200.

Phylaktis, K., and F. Ravazzolo. 2005. *Stock Prices and Exchange Rate Dynamics.* http://papers.ssrn.com/sol3/papers.cfm?abstract_id=251296. Accessed March 14, 2015.

Soenen, L. A., and E. S. Hennigar. 1988. "An Analysis of Exchange Rates and Stock Prices—The US Experience between 1980 and 1986." *Akron Business and Economic Review* (Winter): 7–16.

Annexure

Regression Tables

Table 5 FTSE and GBP/USD

Model	R	R-Squared	Adjusted R-Squared	Std. Error of the Estimate	Change Statistics				
					R-Squared Change	F Change	df1	df2	Sig. F Change
1	.502[a]	.252	.227	.02602	.252	10.111	1	30	.003

a. Predictors: (Constant), GBPUSD
b. Dependent Variable: LOGFTSE

Table 6 ANOVA[b]

Model		Sum of Squares	df	Mean Square	F	Sig.
1	Regression	.007	1	.007	10.111	.003[a]
	Residual	.020	30	.001		
	Total	.027	31			

a. Predictors: (Constant), GBPUSD
b. Dependent Variable: LOGFTSE

Table 7 Coefficients[a]

Model		Unstandardized Coefficients		Standardized Coefficients	t	Sig.
		B	Std. Error	Beta		
1	(Constant)	3.351	.142		23.648	.000
	GBPUSD	.281	.088	.502	3.180	.003

a. Dependent Variable: LOGFTSE

FTSE and GBP/CHF

Model	R	R-Squared	Adjusted R-squared	Std. Error of the Estimate	Change Statistics				
					R-Squared Change	F Change	df1	df2	Sig. F Change
1	.374[a]	.140	.114	.02996	.140	5.517	1	34	.025

a. Predictors: (Constant), GBPCHF
b. Dependent Variable: LOGFTSE

Table 9: ANOVA[b]

Model		Sum of Squares	df	Mean Square	F	Sig.
1	Regression	.005	1	.005	5.517	.025[a]
	Residual	.031	34	.001		
	Total	.035	35			

a. Predictors: (Constant), GBPCHF
b. Dependent Variable: LOGFTSE

Table 10: Coefficients[a]

Model		Unstandardized Coefficients		Standardized Coefficients	t	Sig.
		B	Std. Error	Beta		
1	(Constant)	4.295	.211		20.308	.000
	GBPCHF	-.335	.143	-.374	-2.349	.025

a. Dependent Variable: LOGFTSE

FTSE and GBP/AUD

Model	R	R-Squared	Adjusted R-Squared	Std. Error of the Estimate	Change Statistics				
					R-Squared Change	F Change	df1	df2	Sig. F Change
1	.880[a]	.774	.766	.01402	.774	99.254	1	29	.000

a. Predictors: (Constant), GBPAUD
b. Dependent Variable: LOGFTSE

Table 12: ANOVA[b]

Model		Sum of Squares	df	Mean Square	F	Sig.
1	Regression	.020	1	.020	99.254	.000[a]
	Residual	.006	29	.000		
	Total	.025	30			

a. Predictors: (Constant), GBPAUD
b. Dependent Variable: LOGFTSE

Table 13: Coefficients[a]

Model		Unstandardized Coefficients		Standardized Coefficients	t	Sig.	Collinearity Statistics	
		B	Std. Error	Beta			Tolerance	VIF
1	(Constant)	4.098	.030		138.116	.000		
	GBPAUD	-.180	.018	-.880	-9.963	.000	1.000	1.000

a. Dependent Variable: LOGFTSE

FTSE and GBP/YEN

Model	R	R-Squared	Adjusted R-Squared	Std. Error of the Estimate	Change Statistics				
					R-Squared Change	F Change	df1	df2	Sig. F Change
1	.882[a]	.777	.770	.01391	.777	101.277	1	29	.000

a. Predictors: (Constant), GBPYEN
b. Dependent Variable: LOGFTSE

Table 15: ANOVA[b]

Model		Sum of Squares	df	Mean Square	F	Sig.
1	Regression	.020	1	.020	101.277	.000[a]
	Residual	.006	29	.000		
	Total	.025	30			

a. Predictors: (Constant), GBPYEN
b. Dependent Variable: LOGFTSE

Table 16: Coefficients[a]

Model		Unstandardized Coefficients		Standardized Coefficients	t	Sig.	Collinearity Statistics	
		B	Std. Error	Beta			Tolerance	VIF
1	(Constant)	3.987	.018		216.512	.000		
	GBPYEN	-.001	.000	-.882	-10.064	.000	1.000	1.000

a. Dependent Variable: LOGFTSE

GBP/EURO and FTSE

Model	R	R-Squared	Adjusted R-Squared	Std. Error of the Estimate	Change Statistics				
					R-Squared Change	F Change	df1	df2	Sig. F Change
1	.330[a]	.109	.082	.03050	.109	4.142	1	34	.050

a. Predictors: (Constant), GBPEURO
b. Dependent Variable: LOGFTSE

Table 18: ANOVA[b]

Model		Sum of Squares	df	Mean Square	F	Sig.
1	Regression	.004	1	.004	4.142	.050[a]
	Residual	.032	34	.001		
	Total	.035	35			

a. Predictors: (Constant), GBPEURO
b. Dependent Variable: LOGFTSE

Table 19: Coefficients[a]

Model		Unstandardized Coefficients		Standardized Coefficients	t	Sig.
		B	Std. Error	Beta		
1	(Constant)	4.154	.175		23.773	.000
	GBPEURO	-.292	.144	-.330	-2.035	.050

a. Dependent Variable: LOGFTSE

FTSE and GBP/CAD

Model	R	R-Squared	Adjusted R-Squared	Std. Error of the Estimate	Change Statistics				
					R-Squared Change	F Change	df1	df2	Sig. F Change
1	.930[a]	.865	.860	.01084	.865	185.535	1	29	.000

a. Predictors: (Constant), GBPCAD
b. Dependent Variable: LOGFTSE

Table 21: ANOVA[b]

Model		Sum of Squares	df	Mean Square	F	Sig.
1	Regression	.022	1	.022	185.535	.000[a]
	Residual	.003	29	.000		
	Total	.025	30			

a. Predictors: (Constant), GBPCAD
b. Dependent Variable: LOGFTSE

Table 22: Coefficients[a]

Model		Unstandardized Coefficients		Standardized Coefficients	t	Sig.	Collinearity Statistics	
		B	Std. Error	Beta			Tolerance	VIF
1	(Constant)	4.218	.030		138.389	.000		
	GBPCAD	-.250	.018	-.930	-13.621	.000	1.000	1.000

a. Dependent Variable: LOGFTSE

NASDAQ and Exchange Rate USD

Model	R	R Square	Adjusted R Square	Std. Error of the Estimate	Change Statistics				
					R Square Change	F Change	df1	df2	Sig. F Change
1	.418[a]	.175	.151	.06915	.175	7.202	1	34	.011

a. Predictors: (Constant), GBPUSD
b. Dependent Variable: NASDLOG

Table 24:ANOVA[b]

Model		Sum of Squares	df	Mean Square	F	Sig.
1	Regression	.034	1	.034	7.202	.011[a]
	Residual	.163	34	.005		
	Total	.197	35			

a. Predictors: (Constant), GBPUSD

b. Dependent Variable: NASDLOG

Table 25: Coefficients[a]

Model		Unstandardized Coefficients		Standardized Coefficients	t	Sig.	Collinearity Statistics	
		B	Std. Error	Beta			Tolerance	VIF
1	(Constant)	4.471	.365		12.251	.000		
	GBPUSD	-.612	.228	-.418	-2.684	.011	1.000	1.000

a. Dependent Variable: NASDLOG

CHF

Model	R	R-Squared	Adjusted R-Squared	Std. Error of the Estimate	Change Statistics				
					R-Squared Change	F Change	df1	df2	Sig. F Change
1	.304[a]	.092	.066	.07251	.092	3.464	1	34	.071

a. Predictors: (Constant), CHF

b. Dependent Variable: NASDLOG

Table 27: ANOVA[b]

Model		Sum of Squares	df	Mean Square	F	Sig.
1	Regression	.018	1	.018	3.464	.071[a]
	Residual	.179	34	.005		
	Total	.197	35			

a. Predictors: (Constant), CHF

b. Dependent Variable: NASDLOG

Table 28: Coefficients[a]

	Unstandardized Coefficients		Standardized Coefficients			Collinearity Statistics	
Model	B	Std. Error	Beta	t	Sig.	Tolerance	VIF
1 (Constant)	2.540	.512		4.963	.000		
CHF	.642	.345	.304	1.861	.071	1.000	1.000

a. Dependent Variable: NASDLOG

AUD

				Std. Error of the Estimate	Change Statistics				
Model	R	R-Squared	Adjusted R-Squared		R-Squared Change	F Change	df1	df2	Sig. F Change
1	.936[a]	.876	.873	.02678	.876	240.703	1	34	.000

a. Predictors: (Constant), AUD
b. Dependent Variable: NASDLOG

Table 30: ANOVA[b]

Model		Sum of Squares	df	Mean Square	F	Sig.
1	Regression	.173	1	.173	240.703	.000[a]
	Residual	.024	34	.001		
	Total	.197	35			

a. Predictors: (Constant), AUD
b. Dependent Variable: NASDLOG

Table 31: Coefficients[a]

	Unstandardized Coefficients		Standardized Coefficients			Collinearity Statistics	
Model	B	Std. Error	Beta	t	Sig.	Tolerance	VIF
1 (Constant)	2.683	.052		51.250	.000		
AUD	.488	.031	.936	15.515	.000	1.000	1.000

a. Dependent Variable: NASDLOG

YEN

Model	R	R-Squared	Adjusted R-Squared	Std. Error of the Estimate	Change Statistics				
					R-Squared Change	F Change	df1	df2	Sig. F Change
1	.952[a]	.906	.903	.02338	.906	326.534	1	34	.000

a. Predictors: (Constant), YEN

b. Dependent Variable: NASDLOG

Table 33: ANOVA[b]

Model		Sum of Squares	df	Mean Square	F	Sig.
1	Regression	.178	1	.178	326.534	.000[a]
	Residual	.019	34	.001		
	Total	.197	35			

a. Predictors: (Constant), YEN

b. Dependent Variable: NASDLOG

Table 34: Coefficients[a]

Model		Unstandardized Coefficients		Standardized Coefficients	t	Sig.	Collinearity Statistics	
		B	Std. Error	Beta			Tolerance	VIF
1	(Constant)	2.969	.029		101.568	.000		
	YEN	.003	.000	.952	18.070	.000	1.000	1.000

a. Dependent Variable: NASDLOG

EURO

Model	R	R-Squared	Adjusted R-Squared	Std. Error of the Estimate	Change Statistics				
					R-Squared Change	F Change	df1	df2	Sig. F Change
1	.340[a]	.115	.089	.07160	.115	4.430	1	34	.043

a. Predictors: (Constant), EURO

b. Dependent Variable: NASDLOG

Table 36: ANOVA[b]

Model		Sum of Squares	df	Mean Square	F	Sig.
1	Regression	.023	1	.023	4.430	.043[a]
	Residual	.174	34	.005		
	Total	.197	35			

a. Predictors: (Constant), EURO

b. Dependent Variable: NASDLOG

Table 37: Coefficients[a]

Model		Unstandardized Coefficients		Standardized Coefficients			Collinearity Statistics	
		B	Std. Error	Beta	t	Sig.	Tolerance	VIF
1	(Constant)	2.629	.410		6.411	.000		
	EURO	.709	.337	.340	2.105	.043	1.000	1.000

a. Dependent Variable: NASDLOG

CAD

Model	R	R-Squared	Adjusted R-Squared	Std. Error of the Estimate	Change Statistics				
					R-Squared Change	F Change	df1	df2	Sig. F Change
1	.910[a]	.828	.823	.03154	.828	164.066	1	34	.000

a. Predictors: (Constant), CAD

b. Dependent Variable: NASDLOG

Table 39: ANOVA[b]

Model		Sum of Squares	df	Mean Square	F	Sig.
1	Regression	.163	1	.163	164.066	.000[a]
	Residual	.034	34	.001		
	Total	.197	35			

a. Predictors: (Constant), CAD

b. Dependent Variable: NASDLOG

Table 40: Coefficients[a]

		Unstandardized Coefficients		Standardized Coefficients			Collinearity Statistics	
Model		B	Std. Error	Beta	t	Sig.	Tolerance	VIF
1	(Constant)	2.476	.079		31.156	.000		
	CAD	.608	.047	.910	12.809	.000	1.000	1.000

a. Dependent Variable: NASDLOG

Table 41: Relationship between FTSE 100 with Euro/USD

Summary Output

Regression Statistics	
Multiple R	0.364097
R-Squared	0.132567
Adjusted R-Squared	0.107054
Standard Error	0.040652
Observations	36

ANOVA

	Df	SS	MS	F	Significance F
Regression	1	0.008587	0.008587	5.196104	0.029033
Residual	34	0.056189	0.001653		
Total	35	0.064776			

	Coefficients	Standard Error	t Stat	P-value	Lower 95%	Upper 95%	Lower 95.0%	Upper 95.0%
Intercept	1.533004	0.096141	15.94545	2.39E-17	1.337623	1.728386	1.337623	1.728386
FTSE 100	-3.5E-05	1.52E-05	-2.2795	0.029033	-6.6E-05	-3.8E-06	-6.6E-05	-3.8E-06

Source: (Yahoo Finance 2015; Oanda 2015).

Table 42: Relationship between FTSE 100 with USD/CHF

Summary Output

Regression Statistics

Multiple R	0.393842
R-Squared	0.155112
Adjusted R-Squared	0.130262
Standard Error	0.024382
Observations	36

ANOVA

	df	SS	MS	F	Significance F
Regression	1	0.003711	0.003711	6.242009	0.017473
Residual	34	0.020213	0.000594		
Total	35	0.023923			

	Coefficients	Standard Error	t Stat	P-value	Lower 95%	Upper 95%	Lower 95.0%	Upper 95.0%
Intercept	0.782664	0.057662	13.57326	2.76E-15	0.665481	0.899848	0.665481	0.899848
FTSE 100	2.28E-05	9.13E-06	2.498401	0.017473	4.26E-06	4.14E-05	4.26E-06	4.14E-05

Source: (Yahoo Finance 2015; Oanda 2015).

Table 43: Relationship between FTSE with AUD/USD

Summary Output

Regression Statistics

Multiple R	0.761852
R-Squared	0.580418
Adjusted R-Squared	0.568078
Standard Error	0.044569
Observations	36

ANOVA

	df	SS	MS	F	Significance F
Regression	1	0.093427	0.093427	47.03309	6.77E-08
Residual	34	0.067538	0.001986		
Total	35	0.160964			

	Coefficients	Standard Error	t Stat	P-value	Lower 95%	Upper 95%	Lower 95.0%	Upper 95.0%
Intercept	0.247697	0.105403	2.350004	0.024717	0.033493	0.461902	0.033493	0.461902
FTSE 100	0.000114	1.67E-05	6.858068	6.77E-08	8.05E-05	0.000148	8.05E-05	0.000148

Source: (Yahoo Finance 2015; Oanda 2015).

Table 44: Relationship between NASDAQ 100 with Euro/USD

Summary Output

Regression Statistics

Multiple R	0.225548
R-Squared	0.050872
Adjusted R-Squared	0.022957
Standard Error	0.042524
Observations	36

ANOVA

	df	SS	MS	F	Significance F
Regression	1	0.003295	0.003295	1.822359	0.185952
Residual	34	0.061481	0.001808		
Total	35	0.064776			

	Coefficients	Standard Error	t Stat	P-value	Lower 95%	Upper 95%	Lower 95.0%	Upper 95.0%
Intercept	1.25938	0.041367	30.44435	2.95E-26	1.175313	1.343447	1.175313	1.343447
NSD 100	1.75E-05	1.29E-05	1.349948	0.185952	-8.8E-06	4.37E-05	-8.8E-06	4.37E-05

Source: (Yahoo Finance 2015; Oanda 2015).

Table 45: Relationship between NASDAQ 100 with USD/CHF

Summary Output

Regression Statistics

Multiple R	0.236338
R-Squared	0.055855
Adjusted R-Squared	0.028087
Standard Error	0.025775
Observations	36

ANOVA

	df	SS	MS	F	Significance F
Regression	1	0.001336	0.001336	2.011435	0.165219
Residual	34	0.022587	0.000664		
Total	35	0.023923			

	Coefficients	Standard Error	t Stat	P-value	Lower 95%	Upper 95%	Lower 95.0%	Upper 95.0%
Intercept	0.961404	0.025073	38.34385	1.44E-29	0.910449	1.012359	0.910449	1.012359
NSD 100	-1.1E-05	7.84E-06	-1.41825	0.165219	-2.7E-05	4.81E-06	-2.7E-05	4.81E-06

Source: (Yahoo Finance 2015; Oanda 2015).

Table 46: Relationship between NASDAQ 100 with AUD/USD

Summary Output

Regression Statistics

Multiple R	0.876785
R-Squared	0.768752
Adjusted R-Squared	0.76195
Standard Error	0.033088
Observations	36

ANOVA

	df	SS	MS	F	Significance F
Regression	1	0.123741	0.123741	113.0281	2.38E-12
Residual	34	0.037223	0.001095		
Total	35	0.160964			

	Coefficients	Standard Error	t Stat	P-value	Lower 95%	Upper 95%	Lower 95.0%	Upper 95.0%
Intercept	1.305898	0.032187	40.57199	2.2E-30	1.240486	1.371311	1.240486	1.371311
NSD 100	-0.00011	1.01E-05	-10.6315	2.38E-12	-0.00013	-8.6E-05	-0.00013	-8.6E-05

Source: (Yahoo Finance 2015; Oanda 2015).

www.ingramcontent.com/pod-product-compliance
Lightning Source LLC
Chambersburg PA
CBHW022134170526
45157CB00004B/1875